Original title:
The Purpose of Life (According to My Dog)

Copyright © 2025 Creative Arts Management OÜ
All rights reserved.

Author: Giselle Montgomery
ISBN HARDBACK: 978-1-80566-186-3
ISBN PAPERBACK: 978-1-80566-481-9

## Daily Treats of Happiness

Wagging tails and joyful barks,
Sunshine warming furry parks.
A squirrel hops, oh what a tease,
A chase begins with playful ease.

Bowls of kibble, snacks galore,
Rolling in grass, who could ask for more?
Each belly rub, a gift divine,
In every leap, my heart doth shine.

**Dreams on a Leash**

Adventures await on every street,
With noses twitching, oh what a feat!
Chasing tails, exploring ground,
In every sniff, new joys are found.

A stick to fetch, a frog to chase,
The world's my playground, my happy place.
With a wag and a bark, I spread my cheer,
Every day's magic, let's make it clear!

## Simple Pleasures for the Soul

A nap by the sun, oh blissful dream,
Rolling in mud, I reign supreme.
Fetch the ball, the thrill is real,
No worries here, just my joyful zeal.

A pat on my head, a scratch behind ears,
Sharing my joy, quelling your fears.
With every woof, let laughter reign,
In this simple life, there's only gain.

## Hound's Perspective

I greet the dawn with eager paws,
Chasing shadows and little flaws.
In every corner, adventure waits,
Life's too grand to contemplate fates.

With tongues out wide, we race and run,
Fetching dreams 'neath the shining sun.
In my world, it's fun and play,
With sniffs and barks, let's seize the day!

## Pawsitive Reflections

Chasing tails on sunny days,
With a bark that always plays.
Rolling in the grass so green,
Living life like a big machine.

Food and naps are top delight,
Chasing squirrels in morning light.
Every cuddle's purest bliss,
Count my blessings, not a miss.

## Canine Chronicles

A dog's world is vast and wide,
With a ball and friend beside.
Every stick feels like a treat,
I declare my throne, the seat.

Perks of a wag, tail up high,
Sniffing scents that pass me by.
Every day's a new surprise,
In the yard, I'm king, no lies.

## Every Walk an Adventure

Leashes curled and ready to go,
Exploring paths I've yet to know.
Sniffing stories in the breeze,
Oh, the joy, it's such a tease!

Puddles splashed and mud on paws,
I leap with joy, without a pause.
In the park, I'm wild and free,
Life's a game, come play with me!

## **Snuggles and Sunshine**

Morning rays and lazy sighs,
On the couch, I claim my prize.
Head on your lap, what a treat,
With every hug, my heart skips a beat.

Sunbeams dance upon my fur,
In every snuggle, I find a purr.
Life is simple, love's the key,
Wagging tails, just you and me.

## Serenity on Four Legs

A wagging tail, a happy dance,
Sunshine bright, we take a chance.
Chasing squirrels with joyful glee,
Life is simple, just you and me.

Naps in sunbeams, soft and warm,
Guarding dreams, a calming charm.
With every bark, a laugh resounds,
Love's pure joy in leaps and bounds.

## Exploring Home with a Tail

Around the house, I bound and roam,
A quest for snacks, my second home.
Every corner holds a mystery,
The floor's a stage, it's all for me.

The mailman comes, my heart's delight,
A growl, a bark, I'm ready to fight.
But when he waves, I can't resist,
A friend in uniform, I'm sure I missed!

## Delightful Detours

On walks, I stop to sniff the air,
A leaf, a bug, it's all it takes to care.
Each puddle's splash, a fun retreat,
Life's big treasures lie at my feet.

The park awaits, I zoom with zest,
A game of chase, I'm truly blessed.
With every fetch, my heart will sing,
Joy's the chase, and love's the ring.

## Unconditional Wisdom

I speak in woofs, my heart so true,
Life's a gift, I love you too.
With every paw, I share my cheer,
In messy moments, love is clear.

When days get tough, just fetch a toy,
A wagging tail can bring the joy.
So let's embrace each silly jest,
Together, always, we are blessed.

## A Tail's Whisper

In the grass, I roll and play,
Chasing my tail, oh what a day!
Belly rubs and treats galore,
Life's a game, that's for sure!

Squirrel sightings bring pure cheer,
With a bark, I conquer fear.
Every stick, a treasure found,
Joy unbounded, oh what a sound!

**Fetching Joy from Every Moment**

The ball is tossed, and I take flight,
A blur of fur, oh what a sight!
With every fetch, my heart does soar,
Life's a game, I can't ignore!

A puddle splash, my favorite mess,
Life's simple joys, I do confess.
Rolling in leaves brings such delight,
Chasing shadows into the night!

## Unconditional Paws

Through thick and thin, I stand by you,
With wagging tail, forever true.
A nudge, a lick, I heal your blues,
In every moment, love renews.

You share your fries, and I'm your fan,
Together, we make the perfect plan.
With each cuddle and playful stare,
Life's a treat, we gladly share!

## Chasing Sunbeams and Shadows

In sunlit spots, I stretch and bask,
Every ray, a splendid task.
Chasing shadows with quick delight,
Life's a dance, from morn to night!

The world is huge with smells divine,
I greet each friend, my heart aligns.
With wagging tail and playful glee,
Life's a gift, just you and me!

## Wagging into Wonder

Every morning starts with glee,
A wagging tail, just you and me.
Chasing shadows, leaping high,
Life's a game, oh me, oh my!

Squirrels dart and trees await,
With every bark, I seal my fate.
Rolling in grass, oh what a thrill,
Joyful moments, a perfect fill!

**Finding Peace in Bones**

Digging deep, a treasure hunt,
Underneath the old oak stump.
A buried bone, my sacred prize,
Oh sweet delight that never lies!

Chewing gently while I stare,
At humans fussing without a care.
In my world, it's clear as day,
Bones are bliss, come what may!

## Tales from the Backyard

In the yard, adventures soar,
Chasing leaves, what's not to adore?
Every day's a brand new tale,
As my paws dance, I'll never fail!

A garden gnome, my fiercest foe,
With every bark, I steal the show.
Running wild, the sun's warm kiss,
In my realm, I find pure bliss!

## **Heartbeats and Pawprints**

Soft heartbeats, rhythmic and true,
Pawprints mark where I've been with you.
Snuggled close, your laughter rings,
In our world, happiness springs!

With every wag, I share my cheer,
Life's a treat when you are near.
Through puddles splashed and mud so thick,
Together forever, that's the trick!

## Treats of Wisdom

Chasing tails and sticks, oh what a thrill,
A wagging tail brings laughter, never still.
Each treat a lesson, wrapped in delight,
Life's best moments captured, day and night.

Roll in the grass, make friends with the sun,
Even muddy paws know how to have fun.
A drop of joy with every playful leap,
In all of this chaos, a secret to keep.

## **Woofs of Wonder**

Barking at shadows, what could they be?
Adventure awaits, just wait and see!
A sniff in the breeze, a story now told,
Daily life is magic, never gets old.

Chasing squirrels and dreaming of bones,
Sharing my heart with the people in homes.
Life's full of wonder, and I'm here to play,
With every woof, I brighten the day.

## Lessons from a Loyal Heart

When the doorbell rings, I jump with glee,
Because every visitor's a friend to me.
Loyalty shines in a tail's happy dance,
It's the simple things that give life a chance.

Snuggled up close on a rainy day,
A soft, warm presence, come what may.
Sharing my love, without a single fee,
Life's greatest joy is your company.

## Sniffing Out Happiness

Every corner hides a scent so divine,
Nose to the ground, life's treasures I find.
A scratch on the head, a belly to rub,
Happiness blooms in a warm, fuzzy hub.

The world is a playground, so vast and wide,
I run with a purpose, my tail held with pride.
With each wag I send joy out to the air,
A dog's simple ride brings happiness to share.

## **Echoes of Playtime**

In fields of green, I race so free,
My tail a flag, just you and me.
Chasing squirrels, oh what a sight,
Life's all about the next big fright.

A stick to fetch, I dash and dart,
The simple joys, they steal my heart.
With every leap, I feel alive,
In this grand world, I truly thrive.

**Scented Adventures**

With nose to ground, I track the trails,
A world of scents unveils my tales.
Each whiff, a journey, each paw a quest,
For every sniff brings out my zest.

From dinner scraps to trees so tall,
I sniff my way through it all.
Each aroma tells a secret clue,
What makes this life so fresh and new.

**Embracing Every Sniff**

Through grass and dirt, my nose takes lead,
I find the stories that hearts need.
An acorn here, a puddle there,
Life's tiny wonders, I love to share.

In every breeze, there's magic found,
A fleeting moment, joy unbound.
With each new scent, new friends I greet,
In this wild world, my life's complete.

## Love's Leash

Tangled up in love and play,
A leash that guides me every day.
With you beside, I leap and spin,
In this grand dance, we both win.

Through muddy paws and rainy walks,
Together we share all our talks.
In silly barks and happy sighs,
Life is sweet through puppy eyes.

## **Snouts and Stars**

Licking the sky with my nose,
Chasing dreams where the grass grows.
Every bark a wish to the moon,
Life's a snack, and I'm the saloon.

In shadows I'll dig for my find,
With joy unwrapped, I've got my mind.
A tail that wags at the sight of treats,
Living large in my fluffy feats.

## **Wagging Through the Days**

Sunny days call for a stroll,
Chasing tails is my main goal.
Every squirrel is a potential foe,
But I'll still wag, though I won't let go.

Car rides with the wind in my fur,
Don't forget, I'm a cuddly blur.
Lunch breaks mean more than just play,
I'm here for snacks; that's my way!

## Life as a Game of Fetch

Throw the ball, watch me zoom,
My joy leaps high, filling the room.
Return it quick, or let it be,
A game of patience—joyfully free.

Every toss a fresh delight,
I'll catch it, then wrestle it tight.
Getting muddy, my favorite claim,
In the game of fetch, I'm the name!

## **Reflective Routines**

Same old spot by the door, I'll lay,
Watching the world in my joyous play.
A yawn and stretch as the sun sets,
Life's a series of squeaky bets.

Under stars I'll snuggle down tight,
Chasing dreams and barking at night.
Every wag holds a story to tell,
In simple moments, I find my swell.

## **Whimsical Woofs**

Chasing tails in the sun,
Loving every little run.
Sniffing grass, oh what a thrill,
Each moment brings a barking chill.

Squirrels dart, I must pursue,
With a leap, I think I'm through.
Rolling in mud, oh what a blast,
Life's a game, and I run fast.

## **Barking Up the Right Tree**

With a bark, I declare my reign,
Chasing shadows, feeling no pain.
Fetching sticks, my joy displayed,
In my kingdom, no joy delayed.

Every day's a grand parade,
With every fetch, my worries fade.
Tail wagging, joy's my decree,
Just me and the world, oh so free.

## The Language of Love

A wagging tail is all you need,
With every pat, my heart's a seed.
Naps in sunbeams, love's embrace,
In cuddles, I find my place.

A playful tug on a worn-out shoe,
Bringing laughter to me and you.
With every bark, I speak so clear,
In my eyes, there's only cheer.

## Life in Sniffles

The world's a canvas, smells impart,
Every sniff a work of art.
Rolling in leaves, capturing bliss,
Who knew happiness smelled like this?

Chasing tails and dreams alike,
In every puddle, I take a hike.
Life's a puzzle, full of quirks,
In every nook, my joy lurks.

## **Comfort in the Company**

Wagging tails and fluffy hugs,
Every day's a joyful tug.
Chasing squirrels is a must,
In our bond, we place our trust.

Napping on the sunny grass,
The hours just seem to pass.
With a treat tucked in my paw,
Life's a wonder, full of awe.

Running wild, we share a laugh,
Scratching backs and taking a bath.
Every bark is full of cheer,
In this life, I'm never fear.

## Embracing the Everyday

Morning light, the leash in sight,
Adventure calls, oh what a delight!
Sniffing flowers, chasing bees,
Every moment's sure to please.

Mud puddles and dirty paws,
Life's little quirks have no flaws.
Rolling over, belly up,
Sipping water from my cup.

Watching clouds drift in the sky,
Wondering if they're passing by.
With each day, a brand-new game,
In our hearts, we're never tame.

## Paws and Philosophy

In the park, I ponder deep,
Why do humans love their sleep?
Chasing tails, I seek the truth,
In every bark, I find my proof.

Do they know the thrill of chase?
Or the sheer joy of a warm embrace?
Squirrels teach me all that's wise,
In their antics, laughter lies.

Life's rich lessons taught in barks,
Or through playful, muddy parks.
Philosophy in every wag,
Follow your heart, don't let it lag.

## **Life Is a Game of Fetch**

Throw the ball with all your might,
Chase it down, what a flight!
With a bound and joyous leap,
In this moment, joy runs deep.

Rolling grass, a slide and spin,
Fetch again, let the fun begin!
Retrieve it fast, then back to you,
In this game, we both renew.

Laughter barks as we collide,
Rolling over, side by side.
In this play, we find our glee,
Life's a game, just you and me.

## **Joyful Journeys**

Wagging tails and nose in air,
Chasing squirrels without a care.
Every puddle's like a sea,
Oh, the joy of being free!

Every stick is treasure found,
Rolling in the grass, I'm crowned.
Belly rubs, the ultimate bliss,
Life's a game, and I won't miss!

## **Trust in Tails**

With a wag, I greet the day,
Trust all humans to play.
Food's the goal, let's not pretend,
Here's my heart; let's make amends!

Chasing shadows, racing light,
Everything just feels so right.
Silly faces, goofy grins,
In this life, all love begins!

## Adventures in Joy

Every walk's an epic quest,
Sniffing out the very best.
Butterflies, they lead the way,
Oh, what fun we have each day!

Mud and grass, a perfect blend,
A leap and bound, I must transcend.
Just a pup with a sunny soul,
With each adventure, I feel whole!

## **Life in Slow Motion**

Naps are art, a daily crew,
Sunbeam baths, just me and you.
Chasing dreams in snoozy style,
Finding bliss within a while.

Toys undone, a squeaky mess,
Living life with pure finesse.
In each moment, joy takes flight,
With every tail wag, I feel right!

## Canine Questions

Why chase the mailman with glee?
He brings bills but not treats for me.
Is a squirrel just a fluffy snack?
I ponder this while chasing my wagging tail.

When humans sit, why not join the fun?
They stare at screens, I'll fetch and run.
Dreams of bones and endless play,
Isn't this the best way to spend my day?

Why do they talk and I can't reply?
I bark with joy, they ask me why.
If I could only chew on my thoughts,
I'd resolve so many, like why I'm not caught.

So here I am, chasing dreams and flies,
Finding joy in every surprise.
Life's a game, let's romp and roll,
For doggos know how to fill the soul.

## **Tails of Existence**

Every sniff tells a story untold,
From morning dew to the afternoon gold.
Why is rolling in mud so divine?
To me, it's like sipping the finest wine.

With every bark, I claim my space,
A king on my couch, ruling my place.
Can I nap here? Oh, what a thrill,
In dreams, I catch that robot vacuum still.

Chasing my tail, it's a spin of fate,
Round and round, I can't hesitate.
Is this what they mean by finding peace?
Or just the pursuit of a doggie's lease?

As the sun sets and the day ends,
With wagging tails, my crew and friends.
Together we bark, howl, and play,
In the paws of joy, we find our way.

## Sniffs of Serenity

Morning light spills on the floor,
I stretch and yawn, then seek out more.
Why do they rush? What's the big deal?
I prefer to unwind and enjoy my meal.

A park visit, oh what a thrill,
Chasing leaves, it's a wonderful skill.
Watching humans jog, is it a race?
I just run for the joy, not for first place.

Squirrels up high dance up in the tree,
I bark with envy, oh let me be free!
Yet happiness bubbles in the simplest of games,
A stick, a ball, or chasing my names.

So let's paws and take a breather,
In life's great symphony, I'm the chief believer.
With every wag, my heart sings loud,
In simple joys, I'm forever proud.

## Barking for Joy

Each morning greets as I leap from my bed,
With dreams of adventures dancing in my head.
Why sit in the sun when I can chase flies?
Every moment is magic, oh how time flies!

Why must they go to work all day?
When the backyard calls for a game of play.
I'll guard my turf with a proud little bark,
In my kingdom of grass, I'm the king of the park.

Dinner is served, what a glorious scene,
I wag my tail, for I'm the happy cuisine.
Life's a buffet when you're fluffy and sweet,
A smorgasbord of joy is my favorite treat!

So here's to a life that's happy and bright,
Filled with wagging tails and pure delight.
With every woof, I celebrate this cheer,
In the world of a pup, every day's a year!

## **Whiskered Wonders**

In a patch of sun, I snooze away,
Chasing dreams of bone and play.
Squirrels are mysteries I must outsmart,
They tease my paws, they steal my heart.

A wagging tail is my best tool,
It opens doors, makes me the fool.
Every scratch behind my ear,
Is the treasure I hold dear.

## **Wags and Whys**

Why do humans think they run the show?
I'll fetch the ball, and watch them glow.
All I need is a snack and two,
And endless love to chase us through.

When they say, 'sit,' I give them my eyes,
For treats, I know, are the ultimate prize.
I bark the truth without a doubt,
Happiness is what it's all about!

## **Canine Chronicles**

Oh, the tales I could surely tell,
Of sneaky snacks and when I fell.
The neighbor's cat? A great debate,
I'm always right; just check my gait.

Life's a game of fetch and find,
With muddy paws and a joyful mind.
Eating grass? A gourmet meal,
Each little moment, pure canine zeal.

## **Pawprints on My Heart**

A soft paw on my lap does say,
That love is here, come what may.
Through every leap and each small bark,
We light up life, we spark the dark.

So here's to naps and endless walks,
To silly quirks and joyous talks.
Life is better with wagging friends,
Together we cavort, 'til the fun ends!

## Belly Rubs and Epiphanies

In the sun, I lay so still,
Dreaming of treats and a gentle thrill.
A scratch on my belly, oh what delight,
Life's greatest joy, a furry invite.

Chasing my tail, a whirl of fun,
Each dizzy spin, I'm number one.
Squirrels are high, they think they're slick,
But I'm the pro, with just one trick.

When dinner's served, it's game on true,
Counting down seconds, till I'm fed too.
Every moment's a treasure, great and small,
Belly rubs and food, I want it all!

With a wagging tail and a happy bark,
I cherish each day, just leave a mark.
Love's in the air, a grand ballet,
With paws and laughter, I'll lead the way.

## The Art of Napping

On a warm patch, I find my spot,
With dreams of chasing, I'm ready, why not?
A snooze in the sun, what bliss unbound,
Every soft snore is the sweetest sound.

Behind curtains, I'm stealthy, it's true,
Creep on the couch for a nap or two.
Time stands still when I'm in my zone,
In a world of dreams, I'm the king on my throne.

Tickling my ear with a gentle breeze,
I stretch and sigh, oh life is a tease.
In the land of slumber, I rule supreme,
Bouncing through clouds, in a fluffy dream.

Awake just in time for the dinner bell,
With a wag and a leap, all is well.
Napping is art, it's pure and it's free,
In every doze, there's joy, can't you see?

## A Dog's Guide to Gratitude

Wagging my tail with joy profound,
Every little thing, a treasure I've found.
A sunny day or a bone that's new,
I celebrate life with a bark or two.

Squirrels in trees, oh what a show,
I appreciate the thrill, the racing flow.
Grateful for friends who toss the ball,
Each joyful leap, I'm having a ball!

A scratch on the head, I melt with glee,
Little moments bring maximum spree.
Rolling in grass, feeling alive,
In every snuggle, my heart takes a dive.

So here's my secret, so simple, so bright,
To live for the moment and soak in the light.
With wagging joy, I spread cheer anew,
In my world of gratitude, there's room for you!

## **Joy in the Simple Things**

A stick in the park, oh what a treat,
A world of adventure at my furry feet.
Puddles to splash in, a wild, wet round,
Life's little pleasures are everywhere found.

The scent of the breeze, like magic it whirls,
It dances and twirls with the grass and the curls.
The joy of a bark, so fluffy and bright,
In all of the silly, I find pure delight.

Chasing my shadow, a game that's divine,
In cycles of laughter, the sun starts to shine.
Every new day, I run and I play,
With wagging excitement, I'm ready to stay.

For love that is simple brings happiness true,
In muddy adventures, I find joy anew.
With a wag of my tail and a heart full of cheer,
I'll embrace every moment, every day of the year.

## **A Heart Fully Trained in Love.**


In the sun, I roll and play,
Chasing tails at the break of day.
Every scratch behind my ear,
Brings me joy, that much is clear.

Dinner time is my true bliss,
A plate of treats, I can't resist.
Fetch the ball, then nap so deep,
In dreams of food, I happily leap.

A wagging tail, my flag so bright,
Life's a game, I play it right.
With every bark, my heart does sing,
In furry love, I find my spring.

So here we are, just you and me,
Living life, so wild and free.
With goofy grins, we face each day,
In a world where love's the only play.

## Paws of Wisdom

When the mailman comes to call,
I stand my ground, I am quite tall.
Barking loud is what I do,
Yet inside, I hope he's new.

A squirrel darts across the grass,
My thoughts? How fast can I amass?
It's in the chase I find my glee,
Each leap is wisdom, wild and free.

Every stick is a treasure grand,
Brought home with pride, I understand.
Life's a quest for sticks and bones,
With friends around, I'm never alone.

Nap times are when I ponder deep,
Between my dreams and gentle sleep.
For every woof, I trust my heart,
In silly ways, we make our art.

## Furry Philosophies

What's more profound than a belly rub?
Or finding joy in a tiny tub?
In every paw, there's wisdom stored,
Love's a language we all can afford.

Chasing shadows under the sun,
Every chase is a race for fun.
With a wag, I greet the day,
In my world, only joy is allowed to stay.

The cat might plan a stealthy game,
But I just bark, I'm not ashamed.
Furry hearts know how to play,
With every nudge, we find our way.

From puddles splashed to treats devoured,
In every moment, I feel empowered.
For simple joys, I'll always strive,
In this silly life, I truly thrive.

## **Chasing Happiness**

With every toss, I chase the ball,
That glorious flight, I'm having a ball!
Laughter echoes through the park,
In this bliss, I leave my mark.

A sniff here and a dig there,
Finding treasure is my affair.
Rolling in grass, feeling the breeze,
Nature's joy, it aims to please.

Each cozy spot is a throne of dreams,
Where I scheme and plot my schemes.
A lick, a wiggle, and a bark so loud,
In my heart, I'm forever proud.

Chasing joy, it's what I do,
In every moment, my heart is true.
With my humans, life's a dance,
In every wag, I take my chance.

## **Fido's Fables**

In the sun, I chase my tail,
Barking loud as I set sail.
A squirrel runs, it's quite a show,
With a leap, I steal the glow.

A stick, a prize, I hold it tight,
Bringing joy, oh what a sight!
Tug-of-war, my human screams,
In playful nights, we share our dreams.

Food is good; I eat with glee,
But belly rubs are best, you see.
A nap is where my heart does rest,
To fetch the ball, I am the best.

Life's a game, I play it well,
With joyful barks and wagging tails.
In every moment, I just know,
Happiness is the way to grow.

## **Silhouettes of Contentment**

On the couch, I sprawl with pride,
My humans scratch; I feel the tide.
Sunbeam warms my sleepy face,
In this space, I find my grace.

Chasing toes is such delight,
In the dark, I spring with might.
Zoomies in the living room,
While I stir the evening's gloom.

Dinner time, I do my dance,
With wagging tail, I take my chance.
A crumb or two, my every quest,
Each moment's like a treasure chest.

At the park, I run and leap,
With joyful barks, the world I keep.
Rolling in grass, I hear the call,
In this funny realm, I have it all.

## Leashes of Love

Leash in hand, we stroll the street,
Sniffing every treat I meet.
Oh look, a friend, let's bark and play,
With wagging tails, we own the day.

Puddle jumps and muddy paws,
With every leap, I take applause.
A game of fetch, I lead the way,
With my human, we're here to play.

Food is served, it's time to dine,
The best of all is always mine.
With loving eyes, I do behold,
In this warm heart, my tale is told.

As night falls, I curl up tight,
Dreaming of bones throughout the night.
In every woof, in every tug,
I find my joy, my endless hug.

## The Wisdom in Whispers

In the morning, I stretch and yawn,
Waiting for treats as the day is born.
A gentle nudge brings me to play,
With a wagging tail, I greet the day.

My humans speak, but I just know,
A butterfly's dance puts on a show.
Rolling in grass with the softest sigh,
In every moment, I learn to fly.

The world is vast, filled with cheer,
Each tail wag holds love sincere.
A scratch behind my fuzzy ear,
In that warmth, I lose all fear.

At day's end, we gather close,
Sharing dreams of what we love most.
With laughter, barks, and joyful spins,
In this wild ride, true life begins.

## Paws on the Ground

Chasing squirrels in the park,
I bark and wag with glee,
Rolling in the grass so green,
Life is simple as can be.

Naps in sunbeams on the floor,
Dreams of treats and bones,
If I had a million toys,
I'd still fetch all the stones.

My human thinks of work and time,
But I just think of play,
Every stick's a treasure found,
In my doggy world today.

A bark, a leap, a scratchy back,
It's joy that I pursue,
The world's a great big open space,
With every day's a debut!

## Head in the Clouds

Sometimes I ponder lofty thoughts,
Like, should I chase the cat?
A life of treats and belly rubs,
Well, isn't that where it's at?

The clouds are fluffy, just like me,
I dream of chasing skies,
With every leap, I feel so free,
In doggy wonder, I rise.

Why worry 'bout what's down below?
When sniffing flowers is the way,
I'll float on dreams – a pup's delight,
As squirrels dance and play.

With my nose up high and tail in air,
I'm soaring to the stars,
Oh, life is fun, there's so much flair,
In my world of hopes and barks!

## The Meaning of a Wagging Tail

A wagging tail says all it needs,
It's love wrapped up in fur,
With every swish, it paints a smile,
There's joy in every blur.

Like a flag of happy moments,
It waves through thick and thin,
From meeting new friends at the park,
To cozy nights within.

It tells the world, 'I'm ready, come!'
To games of fetch and chase,
In every wag, a promise made,
To love you in this space.

So when you see a tail go wild,
Just know that life is sweet,
In furry hearts, the truth is found,
So let's wag and stomp our feet!

## Life Lessons from the Backyard

In the backyard, I find my truths,
  Among the flowers and leaves,
Every worm, I know their names,
  Nature's gifts on summer eves.

Digging holes, I find my peace,
  The earth beneath my paws,
A treasure trove of hidden fun,
  Just don't tell Mom! Her flaws!

Sticks are swords of bravery,
  I rule my patch of land,
Jumping high to greet the sky,
  With dirt upon my hand.

Every bark echoes my dreams,
  And every sniff's a plan,
In this kingdom, I reign supreme,
  Oh, isn't life just grand?

**Run Free, Live Happy**

With wind in fur, I dash away,
The world is mine to roam,
Each step a dance of freedom's song,
Nature sings, I'm home.

The trees beckon with playful shade,
And puddles splash with glee,
Life is short, but oh so sweet,
In every bark, I'm free.

Chasing dreams on furry paws,
Each leap's a little cheer,
With laughter in my tail, I know,
It's happiness that's near.

So let's run wild, you and I,
In fields both wide and bright,
For joy is found in every stride,
And love shines most at night!

## **Naps and Dreams**

In a sunny spot, I find my place,
Dreaming of treats and a friendly face.
A tail that wags in the midst of a snooze,
Life's simple joys, I happily choose.

Chasing squirrels in slumber, I leap and dart,
With a wagging tail, I follow my heart.
Oh, what a world in my sleepy scene,
Every doze is a treat—my kingdom, serene.

And if a nap gets interrupted too soon,
I'll yawn and stretch; it's back to my tune.
For every sleepy hour spent in delight,
Is a memory made, soft and bright.

So here's to the naps where big dreams begin,
A life full of love, where I always win.
With my dreams in my paws and the world at my feet,
Every snooze is a victory, oh, life is sweet.

## The Art of Tail Wagging

With a flick and a swish, my tail takes flight,
A language of joy, pure and bright.
Whether greeting a friend or a stranger, I sway,
My tail's busy art brightens the day.

Short bursts of joy in a wag so true,
Each rhythmic thump, a love rendezvous.
In the park, I perform with gusto and grace,
For tail wagging, dear friends, is my happy place.

From corner to corner, my joy unfurls,
Telling the world, I'm here to twirl.
With every wag, I share my delight,
An artist of happiness, always in sight.

So when in doubt, just wag it out,
Let your tail do the talking, without any doubt.
In the world of wagging, all hearts find a way,
Life is a party, come join the play!

## Pawsitive Thinking

When life gets you down, just sniff around,
A patch of grass or a lost toy found.
With my nose to the ground, I ponder and play,
Pawsitive vibes are here to stay.

Why fret about things that cause a frown?
Just chase your tail, round and round!
Every little moment can be turned bright,
With a bark and a wiggle, I take flight.

For every empty bowl, there's a full one near,
And every car ride brings my pals near.
So wag a little harder, let's shake off the gloom,
In my fluffy world, there's always room.

Life's a tug of war, with a rope so strong,
Together we can pull, let's sing our song.
In this furry adventure, we'll always find,
A pawsitive thought to fill our mind.

**Unleashed Joy**

Out in the park, I run free and wild,
The world is my oyster, oh, how I smiled!
With friends by my side, each bark a cheer,
In this grand adventure, there's nothing to fear.

Rolling in grass, feeling cool and clean,
Every leap and bound, like a wild-eyed dream.
The sun on my fur, it's a glorious sight,
Unleashed joy, oh, what a delight!

Chasing after sticks, digging deep in the dirt,
With each pesky squirrel, I give them a flirt.
Life is a burst of wagging excitement,
Every second counts, it's sheer enlightenment.

So let's dance through the puddles, splash in the streams,
With hearts wide open and full of dreams.
In my world of joy, there's no room for dread,
Just a wagging tail and a heart well-fed.

## **Leaping into the Present**

Chasing my tail in the sun,
Wagging my joy, just for fun.
Every moment's a brand new game,
What's that over there? Oh, the same!

A leap here, a bound over there,
Life's a park filled with fresh air.
Paw prints left in the soft ground,
In every heartbeat, pure joy found.

Cuddles and snacks, that's my creed,
Life's full of love, that's all I need.
With a bark so loud, I proclaim,
Every day should be just the same!

So forget your worries and roam,
With a wag of the tail, I'm home.
Here's to living with energy strong,
In my world, we can never go wrong!

## **Digging for Happiness**

In the garden, I scratch and dig,
What I find is a little big.
Bones and treasures buried deep,
In the dirt, I happily leap.

Every hole is a new surprise,
A hidden world before my eyes.
With muddy paws, I scout around,
For joy and mischief, my heart's unbound.

When life gets tough, I just dig more,
Searching for happiness, that's my chore.
A sunny spot and a nap suffice,
Dig deep, my friend, that's my advice!

So grab a shovel and join my spree,
Life's an adventure, come play with me.
In every pit, a giggle awaits,
Digging for joy — it's never too late!

## **Barking Up the Right Tree**

See that squirrel? Oh, what a tease!
Barking loudly, I take the breeze.
Each woof is a hopeful shout,
In my world, there's never doubt.

I race to the trunk, my heart afire,
Squirrels scamper, and I aspire.
What's life without a little chase?
Every bounce brings a smiling face.

The trees, they whisper stories old,
Of adventures brave and laughter bold.
With a keen nose and lots of chat,
I'll find the fun, imagine that!

So let me bark my joyful song,
In this wild world, I belong.
For life is good, with every spree,
Chasing dreams — just follow me!

## The Wisdom of Whiskers

With whiskers twitching, I observe,
Every moment has its curve.
A nap means more than you might think,
Life flows smoother with a wink.

Patience is my fluffy art,
Sometimes just waiting plays the part.
In food or play, I find my way,
Living life with an easy sway.

When the ball rolls, I'm on it fast,
But a scratch behind the ears will last.
Seek out joy with every glance,
In this big world, let's take a chance!

So follow me, my furry friend,
With paws of joy that never end.
In simple things, the truth lies deep,
Whiskers whisper secrets, as we leap!

## A Dog's Delight

Chasing a squirrel, oh what a thrill,
Life's a grand game, with time to kill.
Belly rubs and treats, the finest career,
Why chase the sun? It's already here.

Rolling in grass, with a joyful bark,
The world is my playground, a bright dog park.
With each wagging tail and playful leap,
Who needs deep thoughts? Just dreams to keep.

Naps in the sun, oh what a sight,
Counting my blessings, everything's right.
Fetch is my mantra, joy in my stride,
Together you and I, let's take a ride.

A life full of toys, and muddy paws,
With laughter and love, I make my cause.
Every day's magic, no stress, just fun,
Let's dance through the grass, and soak up the sun.

## Fetching Fulfillment

A ball in my mouth, I'm a happy pup,
Throw it again, come on, don't give up!
Chasing my tail is a form of art,
Every little twist warms up my heart.

Snack in the kitchen? Oh, what a thrill!
I'll give you my best doggy look, what a skill.
From sunny spots to cozy beds,
Life's all about treats, and snoozing heads.

Squirrels make me jump, past the old oak tree,
Life's like a chase, it's just meant to be.
With a friend by my side, life's never a bore,
I'll fetch all your dreams, and bring you much more.

Every bark is a cheer, every wag's a grin,
Living this life, I always win.
So throw me a ball, let's run down the lane,
Together we'll laugh, through sunshine and rain.

## Life Lessons from a Leash

A leash leading me, oh what a guide,
I dash and I dart, with no need to hide.
The world is a feast, every sniff a delight,
Life on the move, it feels so right.

People I meet, all want to pet,
These friendly exchanges, I'll never forget.
A scratch on my back, a smile so wide,
Life's about sharing, with joy as our guide.

Every tree's a mystery, a message to find,
Those pesky old squirrels? They're just out of line!
With you by my side, every walk's a parade,
Life is a journey, with laughter displayed.

Throw in the aroma of dinner's delight,
It's the little things that make tails wag right.
So here's my advice, let's bark and play,
Chase every moment, come join in today!

## Joy in the Simple

Sunshine on fur, a perfect embrace,
A stick in my mouth, it's my favorite place.
Rolling on the grass, oh what pure glee,
Sniffing at flowers, just me being me.

Barking at shadows, a dance full of zest,
Finding new friends, I am truly blessed.
Treats are the treasures that life has in store,
With each little nibble, who could want more?

Chasing my dreams, in puddles galore,
Splashing around, who could ask for more?
Every day's an adventure, come take a look,
In my world of joy, there's no need for a book.

So let's wag our tails, in this simple delight,
With laughter and love, our futures shine bright.
Together we'll wander, side by side in cheer,
Life's all about joy, with you always near.

## **Barking Up Joy**

When I wake up with a bark,
Joy is my favorite mark.
Chasing tails and playful leaps,
Silly dreams and playful creeps.

Every stick a mighty quest,
Every nap, a well-earned rest.
The world spins with wagging tails,
In my heart, adventure sails.

A crumb found beneath the chair,
Oh, the victory we share!
Barking loud to greet the day,
In my kingdom, I will play.

Running free, no cares I find,
Life is simple, oh-so-kind.
Fetch the ball, let laughter reign,
In my world, there's no pain.

## **Swimming in Sunshine**

Sunbeams dance upon my fur,
With every ray, my spirit purrs.
I splash in puddles, what a blast,
A wet nose greeting, shadows cast.

Chasing butterflies, I gleefully run,
Each wag a promise, oh-so-fun.
The warmth of grass beneath my paws,
Life's a game without a pause.

Oh, how blissful to roll on the ground,
In every snuffle, joy is found.
A friendly bark to greet a friend,
Together we can never end.

Swimming through sunshine, bright and bold,
Every hour, a tale untold.
Life's a pool of wagging cheer,
In my world, there's nothing to fear.

## Huggable Moments

Cuddled tight, my favorite place,
Warmth and love in every space.
Gentle scratches behind my ears,
In these moments, all's sincere.

Tail thumping, I'm filled with cheer,
Huggable moments, so crystal clear.
Snoozing by the fire's glow,
Contentment swells, just look at me go.

Loving glances, soft and sweet,
Every hug a joyful treat.
Life's not rushed, it's slow and kind,
In these moments, joys unwind.

With every cuddle, hearts entwine,
In your arms, my spirit shines.
Together we'll chase worries away,
Huggable moments make my day.

## Reflections in a Puddle

Puddles glimmering, what a sight,
I leap and splash with pure delight.
See my face, all muddy charm,
In my world, there's never harm.

Wagging tails beside the stream,
Chasing shadows, living the dream.
A gentle sniff, a joyful leap,
In these reflections, secrets keep.

What's life but a playful splash?
A jump, a roll, a joyful crash.
Every ripple tells a tale,
In my heart, adventures sail.

So here I stand, vibrant and free,
In every puddle, joy's decree.
With a bark and wag, I embrace,
Life's reflections, a joyful chase.

## The Meaning of Play

In grassy fields, we trot with glee,
A simple ball is all I see.
Chasing tails and carefree prance,
Life's a game—let's dance, let's dance.

With mud on paws and sand to snuggle,
Every stick is worth a struggle.
I wag my tail, it's pure delight,
To play all day and sleep at night.

The world's a stage, we fetch our dreams,
In puddles deep, I splash and scream.
A simple bark, a happy sound,
In silly games, true joy is found.

So join my chase, lose all your cares,
Together we'll leap, like dogs on airs.
For life is short, let's play today,
And let the world just fade away.

## Scented Paths to Bliss

Oh, the smells that fill the air!
Each blade of grass, a fragrant flare.
With sniffs so deep, I'm lost in trance,
Life's a treasure, let's take a chance.

From morning dew to sunset's glow,
I chase the scents, to and fro.
Each whiff a story, a joyful trace,
In every corner, my sniffing race.

I dig for bones, I dig for fun,
Each find's a victory, I have won.
With wagging tail and happy bark,
I celebrate adventures in the park.

So come along, let's sniff the day,
Every scent is magic, come what may.
In this big world, let's roam with glee,
For happiness lives in each puppy spree.

## Canine Compass

A nose to ground, I know my way,
I'll lead you through each brand-new day.
With floppy ears and tail held high,
Together we'll soar, oh me, oh my.

Through woods and fields, on trails we roam,
With every leap, we find our home.
In every bark, I point the path,
To joy and chaos, and doggy math.

My compass spins when treats are near,
A tail-wag beacon, so have no fear.
With every twist and turn we take,
Life's an adventure, make no mistake.

So grab my leash, let's wander wide,
With a furry friend right by your side.
We'll chase the sun, for joy we seek,
In every sniff, our spirits speak.

## Bone Deep

A buried bone, my prized delight,
My digging skills bring sheer delight.
In muddy paws, I stake my claim,
Each find is victory, all the same.

With gnawing joy, I savor each chew,
These little treasures keep me true.
I guard them close, oh what a heap,
My love for bones runs very deep.

From squeaky toys to crunchy treats,
Life's best moments, oh how sweet!
With wagging tail, I share my prize,
In every bite, pure happiness lies.

So throw me one; I'll dance with glee,
For life with bones is bliss, you'll see.
Let's make a pact, forever we'll keep,
Chasing joy, bone deep, bone deep.

## A Symphony of Barks

In the park, I raise my voice,
A chorus of barks, oh what a choice!
Squirrels scatter, it's quite a show,
Each bark a note, a tail-wagging flow.

Fetch the stick, oh what delight,
Chasing shadows, bounding in flight.
A symphony of growls, woofs, and yips,
Conducted by me with playful flips.

In the shade, I take my rest,
Dream of treats, I am truly blessed.
Every wag a joyful tune,
Life's a stage beneath the moon.

But when the mailman comes into view,
My symphony bursts forth anew!
With every bark, I stake my claim,
In this funny life, I'm the star of the game!

## Joy Between Meals

Breakfast bowl, I prance with zeal,
Oh joy it brings, that tasty meal!
Snack time waits, my nose in the air,
Between each bite, there's love to share.

The cat walks by, I give a wink,
"Your turn to share; what do you think?"
But then I spot, a crumb on the floor,
My greatest feast, I can't ignore!

Patience is key, just wait and see,
Life is better with food, just like me!
Between each meal, I run and play,
Chasing the joy that brightens my day.

As dinner calls, it's time to bolt,
My heart races, oh what a jolt!
For in the nibbles and playful strife,
I find my joy, the dance of life!

**Furry Reflections**

Mirrored pup, with big brown eyes,
I wonder, do I truly realize?
The wisdom that comes with each waggy tail,
In moments of bliss, I cannot fail.

Chasing my thoughts, I leap with glee,
"Who's that furry friend? Oh, wait, it's me!"
Reflections show, the joy I pursue,
Each paw print a story, both old and new.

In sunbeams I bask, so warm and bright,
Daydreaming of bones, as day turns to night.
Pondering life with a head tilt askew,
Finding the laughter in all that I do.

With each bark and wag, I dance through time,
Translating all life into rhyme.
Furry reflections, oh what a treat,
In laughter and play, my world is complete!

## Heartfelt Howls

Under the moon, I raise my voice,
A heartfelt howl, oh what a choice!
From rooftops high, I serenade the night,
With dreams of treats and playful delight.

In the soft glow, my friends gather near,
With wagging tails, they share their cheer.
Each howl a bonding, a laughter shared,
In this wild world, we're unprepared.

Howling at stars, my heart takes flight,
Each note a sparkle in the dark of night.
Together we stand, with love and play,
Creating joy in every single way.

So here's to the howls, both silly and sweet,
A symphony of friendship, a life so neat!
For in every howl, and bark, and run,
I find the magic; we're all just one!

## The World Through My Dog's Eyes

Socks are treasures I must find,
Each shoe is a throne, oh so divine.
The mailman's a villain in disguise,
I bark loud to protect, I'm wise.

A squirrel is a feast, I must pursue,
Nature's strange dance, a curious view.
Butterflies, oh they must be caught,
In the garden's game, I give it all I've got.

A sunny spot? It's time to nap,
While humans stress, I dream with a yap.
Chewing shoes is my art, don't you see?
Life's greatest joy is just being me.

## Frontiers of Friendship

Fetch is a game we play with glee,
Chasing sticks means you're best to me.
With tongue out and tail wagging wide,
We conquer the yard, side by side.

You bring the treats; I bring the cheer,
In our little world, we have no fear.
In mud and grass, we're true explorers,
With every bark, life's never a bore, sir!

Puppy eyes on you, like stars alight,
Cuddles and kisses, midnight delight.
Through thick and thin, I'll stay right here,
With paws and love, I always steer clear.

## Harmony in Hounds

The sound of my tail makes music loud,
With every wag, I draw a crowd.
Chasing dreams on fluffy clouds,
In sunshine's glow, I'm truly proud.

Dinner time's a concert, oh so sweet,
Watch me dance on my little feet.
Squirrels sing, and birds reply,
In my joyful realm, I soar and fly.

Every bark is a note of cheer,
For human friends, I hold so dear.
In our symphony, we play our part,
Two souls entwined, a joyful heart.

## Bonds Beyond Barks

A leash is a promise; let's go explore,
Together we voyage to distant shores.
In mud puddles, we laugh and splash,
Friendship's a treasure, oh what a stash!

Every belly rub's a soothing balm,
With gentle hands, my heart you calm.
Your laughter's the sound that fills the day,
In each wagging tail, love's here to stay.

I guard the yard, a noble knight,
Chasing shadows that dance in the light.
With snuggles and wet-nosed kisses, we thrive,
In this crazy world, I'm so glad you're alive!

www.ingramcontent.com/pod-product-compliance
Lightning Source LLC
Chambersburg PA
CBHW051653160426
43209CB00004B/886